NONE BUT JESUS

Because you are but a young man, beware of temptations and snares; and above all, be careful to keep yourself in the use of means; resort to good company; and howbeit you be nicknamed a Puritan, and mocked, yet care not for that, but rejoice and be glad, that they who are scorned and scoffed by this godless and vain world, and nicknamed Puritans, would admit you to their society; for I must tell you, when I am at this point as you see me, I get no comfort to my soul by any second means under heaven but from those who are nicknamed Puritans. They are the men that can give a word of comfort to a wearied soul in due season, and that I have found by experience . . .

THE LAST AND HEAVENLY SPEECHES, AND GLORIOUS DEPARTURE, OF JOHN, VISCOUNT KENMURE

NONE BUT JESUS

Selections from the writings of
John Flavel

Venture on Him, venture wholly,
Let no other trust intrude;
None but Jesus
Can do helpless sinners good.
Joseph Hart

THE BANNER OF TRUTH TRUST

THE BANNER OF TRUTH TRUST
3 Murrayfield Road, Edinburgh EH12 6EL, UK
P.O. Box 621, Carlisle, PA 17013, USA

*

© Banner of Truth Trust 2014

ISBN:
Print: 978 1 84871 407 6
EPUB: 978 1 84871 408 3
Kindle: 978 1 84871 409 0

*

Typeset in 10.5 / 13.5 pt Adobe Caslon Pro
at the Banner of Truth Trust, Edinburgh

Printed in the USA by
Versa Press, Inc.,
East Peoria, IL

Christ is bread to the hungry, water to the thirsty, a garment to the naked, healing to the wounded, and whatever a soul can desire is found in him.

JOHN FLAVEL

INTRODUCTION

This book contains 384 extracts from the writings of the Nonconformist John Flavel (1627-91). Although his name has been obscure for many years, there has been a recent wave of renewed appreciation for this minister of the gospel. Flavel was a pastor and author who, for the better part of his ministry, laboured in a coastal town in Devon. After studying at University College, Oxford, he began working as a Presbyterian minister in 1650. Six years into his ministry he removed to Dartmouth, and, due to the intermittent legality of Nonconformist ministerial activities, he was permitted to labour sporadically and often clandestinely. So strongly did he sense a divine calling to remain in Dartmouth that twice in his career he refused offers of more lucrative livings in order that he might continue his work amongst 'his poor people in Dartmouth'. Perhaps it was this admirable devotion to his humble flock that ultimately caused his influence to have a ripple effect in ever-widening circles for the following 350 years. Flavel had a deep impact on numerous figures, including George Whitefield, Jonathan Edwards, John Wesley, Charles Spurgeon, U.S. President John Adams, Benjamin Franklin, and Samuel Sewall. Flavel's various writings have been reprinted more than 720 times between 1664 and the present day.

Through the course of completing a doctoral thesis on Flavel's theology I found myself poring over his writings in a search for material which would assist my argument. The aim of the researcher is to lead one's materials in a profitable and useful direction. To my surprise and delight it was, rather, Flavel who led me to the throne of God time and time again. It was on such occasions that I put my pen down and worshipped the Lord of glory.

Having been deeply influenced by *The Loveliness of Christ* (the Banner of Truth Trust), which contains extracts from Samuel Rutherford's *Letters*, it seemed appropriate to do the same with the writings of Flavel. 'He scatters pearls and diamonds with both hands' was the praise that Spurgeon gave to the writings of another of the Puritans, Richard Sibbes, and we could well say the same thing about Flavel. The quotations in this book are drawn out of Flavel's six-volume *Works* (also published by the Banner of Truth Trust), and cover topics such as providence, the excellency of Christ, heaven, conversion, suffering, and glory. A short glossary of several archaic words is also provided at the end of the text.

My only hope for this book is that through these 'gems,' many would feast their hearts on Jesus Christ, the great God and Saviour of John Flavel. If the reader gets even a fraction of the benefit that I received from Flavel's *Works* whilst buried deep in the library, it will be well worth the effort.

NATHAN T. PARKER
Durham, England
2013

Dedicated to my Dad,

JIM PARKER.

Thank you for the greatest gift in the world—being a godly father and example.

Thank you also for introducing me to John Flavel.

NONE BUT JESUS

Christ shall be the centre to which all the lines of my ministry shall be drawn. I have spoken and written of many other subjects in my sermons and epistles, but it is all *reductively* the preaching and discovery of Jesus Christ: of all the subjects in the world, this is the sweetest; if there be any thing on this side of heaven worthy our time and studies, this is it.[1]

---

[1] The Fountain of Life, I:33.

It is greatly to your loss, that you live at such a distance from God, and are so seldom with him; think not the ablest ministers, or choicest books will ever be able to satisfy your doubts and comfort your hearts, whilst you let down your communion with God to so low a degree.[2]

The whole world is not a theatre large enough to display the glory of Christ upon: or unfold the one half of the unsearchable riches that lie hidden in him. These things will be far better understood, and spoken of in heaven, by the noon-day divinity, in which the immediately illuminated assembly do there preach his praises, than by such a stammering tongue, and scribbling pen as mine, which doth but mar them. Alas! I write his praises but by moon-light; I

[2] England's Duty, IV:263.

cannot praise him so much as by halves. What shall I say of Christ? The excelling glory of that object dazzles apprehension and swallows up all expression. When we have borrowed metaphors from every creature that hath any excellency or lovely property in it, till we have stripped the whole creation bare of all its ornaments, and clothed Christ with all that glory; when we have worn our tongues to the stumps in ascribing praises to him; alas! we have still done nothing, when all is done.[3]

New wonders will appear in Christ, if we behold him to eternity.[4]

And such is the *deliciousness* of this subject, that were there ten thousand volumes

[3] Fountain of Life, I:xviii.
[4] Twelve Sacramental Meditations, VI:414.

written upon it, they would never cloy, or become nauseous to a gracious heart. We used to say *one thing* tires, and it is true that it doth so, except that one thing be virtually and eminently all things, as Christ is; and then one thing can never tire; for such is the variety of sweetness in Christ.[5]

God allows his children to complain *to* him, but not *of* him.[6]

Away to thy God, poor Christian, get thee into thy closet, pour out thy soul before him; and that ease which thou seekest in vain elsewhere, will there be found, or nowhere.[7]

[5] Fountain of Life, I:23.
[6] The Balm of the Covenant, VI:132.
[7] England's Duty, IV:254.

Though all other things do, yet Christ neither doth, nor can grow stale. The blood of Christ doth never dry up. He is the same yesterday, today, and forever. As his body in the grave saw no corruption, so neither can his love, or any of his excellencies. When the saints shall have fed their eyes upon him in heaven thousands and millions of years, he shall be as fresh, beautiful, and orient as at the beginning. Other beauties have their prime, and their fading time; but Christ abides eternally. Our delight in creatures is often most at first acquaintance; when we come nearer to them, and see more of them, the edge of our delight is abated: but the longer you know Christ, and the nearer you come to him, still the more do you see of his glory. Every farther prospect of Christ entertains the mind with a fresh delight. He is as it were a new Christ every day, and yet the same Christ still.[8]

A drop of grace is better than a sea of gifts.[9]

The faith that receives the righteousness of Christ may be very different in degrees of strength, but the received righteousness is equal upon all believers: a piece of gold is as much worth in the hand of a child, as it is in the hand of a man. O the exceeding preciousness of saving faith![10]

Mercy and pardon are designed for, and bestowed upon, the greatest and vilest of sinners to enhance and raise the glory of

---

[8] Fountain of Life, I:270.
[9] Fountain of Life, I:294.
[10] The Method of Grace, II:437.

free grace to the highest pitch. God picks out such sinners as you are, on purpose to illustrate the glory of his grace in and upon you: he knows that you, to whom so much is forgiven, will love much (*Luke* 7:47).[11]

This care of God, thus engaged for you, is your convoy to accompany and secure you till it see you safe into your harbour of eternal rest.[12]

Many of those who are sincere in their profession, and do arrive at last, yet come to heaven (as I may say) by the gates of hell; and put in, as a poor weather-beaten vessel comes into the harbour, more like a wreck than a ship, neither mast nor sail left. The

[11] England's Duty, IV:154-5.
[12] The Righteous Man's Refuge, III:390.

righteous themselves are scarcely saved, *i.e.*, they are saved with very much difficulty.[13]

We measure the good and evil of providences by their respect to the ease and pleasure of our flesh.[14]

It is a poor comfort to have an increasing estate, and a dead and declining soul.[15]

We should call our hearts to account every evening, and say, O my heart! Where hast thou been today? Where have thy thoughts been wandering? Where hast thou made a road today? O naughty heart! Vain heart! couldst thou not abide by the

[13] Navigation Spiritualized, V:288.
[14] Balm of the Covenant, VI:99.
[15] The Seaman's Companion, V:395.

fountain of delights? Is there better entertainment with the creature than with God?[16]

The lamp of life is almost burnt down, the glass of time almost run; yet a few, a very few days and nights more, and then time, nights and days shall be no more.[17]

O when thou goest to God in any duty, take thy heart aside, and say, O my soul, I am now addressing myself to the greatest work that ever a creature was employed about: I am going into the awful presence of God about business of everlasting moment.[18]

[16] A Saint Indeed, V:505.
[17] A Treatise of the Soul of Man, II:586.
[18] A Saint Indeed, V:464.

Let not them that are at the top of the world be lifted up; nor those that are at the bottom be dejected.[19]

A saving, though an immethodical knowledge of Christ, will bring us to heaven (*John* 17:2) but a regular and methodical, as well as a saving knowledge of him, will bring heaven into us (*Col.* 2:2-3).[20]

It is true, some wicked men die in seeming peace, and some good men in trouble, but both the one and the other are mistaken: the first, as to the good estate he fancies himself in, and the other as to his bad estate; and a few moments will clear up the mistake of both.[21]

[19] A Sermon Preached at the Funeral of John Upton, VI:136.
[20] Fountain of Life, I:21.
[21] England's Duty, IV:297.

Light is a special help to obedience, and obedience is a singular help to increase your light.[22]

He himself was deserted of God for a time, that they might not be deserted forever.[23]

Repentance will cost you more than a few cheap words against sin.[24]

Herein the admirable grace of this heavenly suitor appears, that Jesus Christ passed by millions of creatures of more excellent gifts and temperaments, and never makes them one offer of himself; never turneth aside to give one knock at their door: but

---

[22] Fountain of Life, I:143.
[23] Method of Grace, II:247.
[24] Method of Grace, II:62.

comes to thee, the vilest and basest of creatures, and will not be gone from thy door without his errand's end.[25]

Christ's bringing home of all believers unto God, will be matter of unspeakable joy to themselves. For whatever knowledge and acquaintance they had with God here, whatever sights of faith they had of heaven and the glory to come in this world, yet the sight of God and Christ the Redeemer will be an unspeakable surprise to them in that day. This will be the day of relieving all their wants, the day of satisfaction to all their desires: for now they are come where they would be, arrived at the very desire of their souls.[26]

---

[25] England's Duty, IV:127.
[26] Method of Grace, II:283.

Redeemed souls must expect no rest or satisfaction on this side of heaven, and the full enjoyment of God. The life of a believer in this world is a life of motion and expectation: they are now coming to God (*1 Pet.* 2:4). God, you see, is the centre and rest of their souls (*Heb.* 4:9). As the rivers cannot rest till they pour themselves into the bosom of the sea, so neither can renewed souls find rest till they come into the bosom of God.[27]

Death, to the saints, is the door by which they enter into the enjoyment of God: the dying Christian is almost at home, yet a few pangs and agonies more, and then he is come to God, in whose presence is the fulness of joy. The same day we loose from this shore, we shall be landed upon the blessed

[27] *Method of Grace*, II:284.

shore, where we shall see and enjoy God for ever.[28]

Learn from [death] the vanity of the creature, the emptiness, and nothingness of the best things here below.[29]

The keeping and right managing of the heart in every condition, is the great business of a Christian's life.[30]

Oh, for a better heart! Oh for a heart to love God more! To hate sin more, to walk more evenly with God: Lord, deny not to me such a heart, whatever thou deny me; give me a heart to fear thee, love and delight in thee.[31]

[28] Method of Grace, II:284-5.
[29] Funeral of John Upton, VI:130.
[30] A Saint Indeed, V:425.
[31] A Saint Indeed, V:427.

He indeed is rich in grace, whose graces
are not hindered by his riches.[32]

Know further for thy comfort, that God
would never leave thee under so many
heart-troubles and burdens, if he intended
not thy real benefit thereby. Thou art often
crying out: Lord! Why is it thus? Why go
I mourning all the day, having sorrow in
my heart? Thus long have I been exercised
with hardness of heart, and to this day have
not obtained a broken heart. Many years
have I been praying and striving against
vain thoughts, yet am I still infested and
perplexed with them. O when shall I get
a better heart! I have been in travail, and
brought forth but wind. I have obtained no
deliverance, neither have the corruptions of
my heart fallen. I have brought this heart

[32] A Saint Indeed, V:438.

many times to prayers, sermons and sacraments, expecting and hoping for a cure from them, and still my sore runneth, and ceaseth not. Pensive soul! Let this comfort thee; thy God designs thy benefit, even by these occasions of thy sad complaints. For, (1) Hereby he would let thee see what thy heart by nature is and was, and therein take notice how much thou art beholden to free grace. He leaves thee under these exercises of spirit, that you mayest lie, as with thy face upon the ground, admiring that ever the Lord of glory should take such a toad; so vile a creature into his bosom. Thy base heart, if it be good for nothing else, yet serves to commend and set off, the unsearchable riches of free grace. (2) This serves to beat thee off continually from resting, yea, or but glancing upon thine own righteousness or excellency. The corruption of thy heart, working in all thy duties, makes thee sensible to feel that the bed is too short, and the covering too narrow. Were it not for those reflections thou hast after duties, upon the dullness and distractions of thine heart in them; how apt wouldst thou be to fall in love with, and admire thine own performances and enlargements? For if notwithstanding these, thou hast much to do with the pride of thy heart, how much more, if such humbling and self-abasing considerations were wanting? (3) And lastly, this tends to make thee the more compassionate and tender towards others: perhaps thou wouldst have little pity for the distresses and soul troubles of others, if thou hadst less experience of thine own.[33]

[33] A Saint Indeed, V:508.

The heart of man is his worst part before it be regenerate, and the best afterwards: it is the seat of principles, and the fountain of actions. The eye of God is, and the eye of the Christian ought to be, principally fixed upon it. The greatest difficulty in conversion is to win the heart *to* God and the greatest difficulty after conversion is to keep the heart *with* God. Here lies the very pinch and stress of religion; here is that that makes the way to life a narrow way, and the gate of heaven a straight gate.[34]

O how many have been coached to hell in the chariots of earthly pleasures, while others have been whipped to heaven by the rod of affliction?[35]

[34] A Saint Indeed, V:423.
[35] A Saint Indeed, V:438.

Let none but the servants of sin be the slaves of fear, let them that have delighted in evil, fear evil.[36]

A lion at liberty is terrible to meet, but who is afraid of the lion in the keeper's hand?[37]

To shuffle over religious duties with a loose and heedless spirit will cost no great pains; but to set thyself before the Lord, and tie up thy loose and vain thoughts to a constant and serious attendance upon him: this will cost thee something. To attain a facility and dexterity of language in prayer, and put thy meaning into apt and decent expressions is easy, but to get thy heart broken for sin whilst thou art confessing

[36] A Saint Indeed, V:450.
[37] A Saint Indeed, V:451.

it; melted with free grace, whilst thou art blessing God for it; to be really ashamed and humbled through the apprehensions of God's infinite holiness, and to keep thy heart in this frame, not only in, but after duty; will surely cost thee some groans, and travailing pain of soul. To repress the outward acts of sin, and compose the external part of thy life in a laudable and comely manner is no great matter—even carnal persons by the force of common principles can do this—but to kill the root of corruption within, to set and keep up an holy government over your thoughts, to have all things lie straight and orderly in the heart, this is not easy.[38]

Remember that this God, in whose hand all the creatures are, is your Father, and is

[38] A Saint Indeed, V:428.

much more tender over you than you are or can be over yourselves: 'He that toucheth you, toucheth the apple of mine eye' (*Zech.* 2:8).[39]

Thou sayest, do what I can, yet I cannot keep my heart with God. Soul, if thou dost what thou canst, thou hast the blessing of an upright heart, though God sees good to exercise you under the affliction of a dis-composed heart. There remains still some wildness in the thoughts and fancies of the best to humble them.[40]

The improvement of our graces depends upon the keeping our hearts; I never knew grace thrive in a negligent and careless soul: the habits and roots of grace are planted in

[39] A Saint Indeed, V:451.
[40] A Saint Indeed, V:431.

the heart; and the deeper they are radicated there, the more thriving and flourishing grace is.[41]

The careless heart makes nothing out of any duty or ordinance it performs or attends on, and yet these are the conduits of heaven from where grace is watered and made fruitful: a man may go with an heedless spirit from ordinance to ordinance, abide all his days under the choicest teachings and yet never be improved by them; for heart neglect is a leak in the bottom, no heavenly influences how rich soever, abide in that soul (*Matt.* 13:3-4).[42]

Though God hath reserved to himself a liberty of afflicting his people, yet he hath tied up his own hands by promise never to

[41] A Saint Indeed, V:435.
[42] A Saint Indeed, V:436.

take away his loving-kindness from them. O my heart, my haughty heart! Dost thou well to be discontented, when God hath given thee the whole tree, with all the clusters of comfort growing on it, because he suffers the wind to blow down a few leaves? Indeed, if he had cut off his love, or discovenanted my soul, I had reason to be cast down; but this he hath not, nor can he do it.[43]

Not a creature moves hand or tongue against thee, but by his permission.[44]

As God did not at first choose you because you were high, so he will not forsake you because you are low.[45]

---

[43] A Saint Indeed, V:441-2.
[44] A Saint Indeed, V:442.
[45] A Saint Indeed, V:442.

When providence hath blasted your estates, your summer friends may grow strange, as fearing you may be troublesome to them; but will God do so? No, no! 'I will never leave thee, nor forsake thee' (*Heb.* 13:5). Indeed if adversity and poverty could bar you from access to God, it were a sad condition; but you may go to God as freely as ever.[46]

You lie too near his heart to hurt you. Nothing grieves him more than your groundless and unworthy suspicions of his designs do. Would it not grieve a faithful, tender-hearted physician when he hath studied the case of his patient, and prepared the most excellent recipes to save his life to hear him cry out; 'O he hath undone me, he

---

[46] A Saint Indeed, V:442.

hath poisoned me!'; because it gripes and pains him in the operation?[47]

It would much stay the heart under adversity to consider that God, by such humbling providences may be accomplishing the thing for which you have long prayed and waited. And should you be troubled at that? Say Christian, hast thou not offered many prayers to God such as these: that he would keep thee from sin, discover to thee the emptiness and insufficiency of the creature; that he would kill and mortify thy lusts, that thy heart may never find rest in any enjoyment but Christ? Why now, by such humbling and impoverishing strokes, God may be fulfilling thy desire.[48]

[47] A Saint Indeed, V:442.
[48] A Saint Indeed, V:443.

Is it not enough that God is so gracious to do *what* thou desirest, but thou must be so impudent to expect he should do it *in the way* which thou prescribest?[49]

Mourners you may, and ought to be; but self-tormentors you must not be. Complain to God you may, but to complain of God—though but by an unsuitable carriage, and the language of your actions—you must not.[50]

Luther, in his last will and testament hath this expression, 'Lord thou hast given me wife and children, I have nothing to leave them, but I commit them unto thee.'[51]

Settle this great truth in your hearts, that no trouble befalls Zion, but by the

[49] A Saint Indeed, V:443.
[50] A Saint Indeed, V:446.
[51] A Saint Indeed, V:494.

permission of Zion's God; and he permits nothing out of which he will not bring much good at last to his people.[52]

Well then, as Luther told Melanchthon, *Desinat Philippus esse rector mundi;* so say I to you; Let infinite wisdom, power, and love alone; for by these all creatures are swayed, and actions guided, in reference to the church; it is none of our work to rule the the world, but to submit to him who doth.[53]

Fear is both a multiplying and a tormenting passion; it represents troubles much greater than they are, and so tortures and wracks the soul much worse than when the suffering itself comes.[54]

[52] A Saint Indeed, V:446.
[53] Latin: 'Philip, stop being the the governor of the world!' A Saint Indeed, V:447.
[54] A Saint Indeed, V:453.

Quiet your trembling hearts by recording and consulting your past experiences of the care and faithfulness of God in former distresses. These experiences are food for your faith in a wilderness condition.[55]

For though I confess poverty hath its temptations as well as prosperity, yet I am confident prosperity hath not these excellent advantages that poverty hath: for here you have an opportunity to discover the sincerity of your love to God, when you can live upon him, find enough in him, and constantly follow him, even when all external inducements and motives fail.[56]

As soon as the body is dead, the gracious soul is swallowed up in life (*Rom.* 8:10-11). When once you have loosed from this

[55] A Saint Indeed, V:454.
[56] A Saint Indeed, V:463.

shore, in a few moments, your souls will be wafted over upon the wings of angels to the other shore of a glorious eternity.[57]

Sometimes the duty is almost ended before their hearts begin to stir to feel any warmth, quickening, or power from it; but all this while the prepared heart is at its work. This is he that ordinarily gets the first sight of Christ in a sermon, the first seal from Christ in a sacrament, the first kiss from Christ in secret prayer. I tell you, and I tell you but what I have felt, that prayers and sermons would appear to you other manner of things than they do, did you but bring better ordered hearts unto them; you would not go away dejected and drooping.[58]

[57] A Saint Indeed, V:491.
[58] A Saint Indeed, V:500.

The heart is a hungry and restless thing; it will have something to feed upon. If it enjoy nothing from God, it will hunt for something among the creatures, and there it often loses itself, as well as its end. There is nothing more engages the heart to a constancy and evenness in walking with God, than the sweetness which it tastes therein.[59]

When the waters of relief run low, and want begins to pinch hard, how prone are the best hearts to distrust the fountain! When the meal in the barrel and the oil in the cruse are almost spent, our faith and patience are almost spent too. Now it is difficult to keep down the proud and unbelieving heart in an holy quietude and sweet submission at the foot of God. It is an easy thing to talk of trusting God for

[59] A Saint Indeed, V:506.

daily bread while we have a full barn or purse, but to say as the prophet (*Hab.* 3:17), '*Though the fig-tree should not blossom, neither fruit be in the vine, etc., yet will I rejoice in the Lord*': surely this is not easy.[60]

It will signify more to my comfort to spend one solitary hour in mourning before the Lord over heart corruption, than many hours in a seeming zealous, but really dead performance of common duties with the greatest enlargements and richest embellishments of parts and gifts. By this very thing Christ distinguishes the formal and serious Christian (*Matt.* 6:5). The one is for the street and synagogue, for the observation and applause of men, but the other is a closet-man. He drives on a home-trade, a heart-trade.[61]

[60] A Saint Indeed, V:457.
[61] A Saint Indeed, V:507.

Never be troubled then for the want of those things that a man may have and be eternally damned; but rather bless God for that which none but the favourites and darlings of heaven have.[62]

Many a one is now in hell that had a better head than thine, and many a one now in heaven that complained of as bad a heart as thine.[63]

God will shortly put a blessed end to all these troubles, cares, and watchings. The time is coming, when thy heart shall be as thou wouldst have it, when thou shalt be discharged of all these cares, fears, and sorrows, and never cry out: O my hard, my proud, my vain, my earthly heart any more! When all darkness shall be banished

[62] A Saint Indeed, V:507-8.
[63] A Saint Indeed, V:508.

from thine understanding, and thou shalt clearly discover all truths in God, that crystal ocean of truth: when all vanity shall be purged perfectly out of thy thoughts, and they be everlastingly, ravishingly, and delightfully entertained and exercised upon that supreme goodness, and infinite excellency of God, from whom they shall never start any more like a broken bow.[64]

It is as hard for some to look upon other men's gifts without envy, as it is to look upon their own without pride.[65]

The merciful Lord Jesus, by his admirable patience and bounty hath convinced you, how loth he is to leave, or lose you. To this day his arms are stretched forth to gather you, and will you not be gathered?

---

[64] A Saint Indeed, V:508-9.
[65] Fountain of Life, I:24.

Alas for my poor neighbours! Must so many of them perish at last? Lord, by what arguments shall people be persuaded to be happy?[66]

Remember, death will shortly break up all your families and disband them.[67]

Look to it, my dear friends, that none of you be found Christless at your appearance before him. Those that continue Christless now, will be left speechless then.[68]

There is no doctrine more excellent in itself, or more necessary to be preached and studied, than the doctrine of Jesus Christ, and him crucified.[69]

[66] Fountain of Life, I:28.
[67] Fountain of Life, I:29.
[68] Fountain of Life, I:30.
[69] Fountain of Life, I:34.

The knowledge of Jesus Christ is the very marrow and kernel of all the Scriptures; the scope and centre of all divine revelations: both Testaments meet in Christ.[70]

The knowledge of Christ is profound and large. All other sciences are but shadows; this is a boundless, bottomless ocean. Though something of Christ be unfolded in one age, and something in another, yet eternity itself cannot fully unfold him.[71]

The sufficiency of the doctrine of Christ makes men wise unto salvation. A little of this knowledge, if saving and effectual upon thy heart, will do thy soul more service than all the vain speculations, and profound parts that others so much glory

[70] Fountain of Life, I:34.
[71] Fountain of Life, I:36.

in. Poor Christian, be not dejected because thou seest thyself out-stripped and excelled by so many in other parts of knowledge. If thou know Jesus Christ thou knowest enough to comfort and save thy soul. Many learned philosophers are now in hell, and many illiterate Christians in heaven.[72]

That is the best sermon that is most full of Christ, not of art and language. I know that a holy dialect well becometh Christ's ministers, they should not be rude and careless in language or method; but surely the excellency of a sermon lies not in that, but in the plainest discoveries and liveliest applications of Jesus Christ.[73]

Study to know Christ more intensively, to get the experimental taste, and lively

[72] Fountain of Life, I:38.
[73] Fountain of Life, I:39.

power of his knowledge upon your hearts and affections. This is the knowledge that carries all the sweetness and comfort in it. Christian, I dare appeal to thy experience, whether the experimental taste of Jesus Christ, in ordinances and duties, has not a higher and sweeter relish than any created enjoyment thou ever tastedst in this world? O then, separate, devote, and wholly give thyself, thy time, thy strength to this most sweet transcendent study.[74]

It is our calling, as the Bridegroom's friends, to woo and win souls to Christ, to set him forth to the people as crucified among them (*Gal.* 3:1), to present him in all his attractive excellencies, that all hearts may be ravished with his beauty, and charmed into his arms by love.[75]

[74] Fountain of Life, I:39-40.
[75] Fountain of Life, I:40.

Your time and gifts are not yours, but God's.[76]

God, you know, is the fountain, ocean, and centre of all delights and joys.[77]

Take heed that you rest not satisfied with that knowledge of Christ you have attained, but grow on towards perfection. It is the pride and ignorance of many professors when they have got a few raw and undigested notions, to swell with self-conceit of their excellent attainments. And it is the sin, even of the best of saints, when they see how deep the knowledge of Christ lies, and what pains they must take to dig for it, to throw by the shovel of duty, and cry, *Dig we cannot.* To your work Christians,

[76] Fountain of Life, I:41.
[77] Fountain of Life, I:46.

to your work; let not your candle go out: sequester yourselves to this study. Count all therefore but dross in comparison of that excellency which is in the knowledge of Jesus Christ.[78]

Christ is the great favourite in heaven: his image upon your souls, and his name in your prayers, makes both accepted with God.[79]

How worthy is Jesus Christ of all our love and delights? You see how infinitely the Father delighteth in him, how he ravishes the heart of God; and shall he not ravish our hearts? I present you a Christ this day, able to ravish any soul that will but view and consider him. O that you did but see this lovely Lord, Jesus Christ! Then

[78] Fountain of Life, I:42.
[79] Fountain of Life, I:50.

you would go home love-sick: surely he is a drawing Saviour (*John* 12:32). Why do ye lavish away your precious affections upon vanity? None but Christ is worthy of them: when you spend your precious affections upon other objects, what is it but to dig for dross with golden mattocks? The Lord direct our hearts into the love of Christ. O that our hearts, loves and delights might meet and concentre with the heart of God in this most blessed object! O let him that left God's bosom for you, be embosomed by you, though yours be nothing to God's; he that left God's bosom for you, deserves yours.[80]

Happy were it, if puzzled and perplexed Christians would turn their eyes from the defects that are in their own obedience, to

[80] Fountain of Life, I:50.

the fulness and completeness of Christ's obedience; and see themselves complete in him, when most lame and defective in themselves.[81]

What was debt to Christ, is grace to us. What an ancient friend God hath been to us.[82]

God has given Christ as bread to poor starving creatures, that by faith they might eat, and live.[83]

As your good was Christ's end, so let his glory be your end.[84]

O brethren, let not the feet of your conversation be as the feet of a lame man,

---

[81] Fountain of Life, I:59.
[82] Fountain of Life, I:60.
[83] Fountain of Life, I:66.
[84] Fountain of Life, I: 101.

which are unequal (*Prov.* 26:7). Be not
sometimes hot, and sometimes cold; at one
time careful, at another time careless; one
day in a spiritual rapture, and the next, in a
fleshly frolic.[85]

In the name *Jesus* the whole gospel is
contained.[86]

As an umpire or arbitrator; one that layeth his hands upon both parties, so doth
Christ. He layeth his hands (speaking after
the manner of men) upon God, and saith,
Father, wilt thou be at peace with them,
and re-admit them into thy favour? If thou
wilt, thou shalt be fully satisfied for all that
they have done against thee. And then he
layeth his hand upon man, and saith, Poor

[85] Fountain of Life, I:105.
[86] Fountain of Life, I:108.

sinner, be not discouraged, thou shalt be justified and saved.[87]

Christ came to impart the mind of God to us.[88]

Let Christ have the whole glory of your recovery ascribed to him. It is highly reasonable that he that laid down the whole *price*, should have the whole *praise*.[89]

Light is a special help to obedience, and obedience is a singular help to increase your light.[90]

There is much folly in the best of our duties, we know not how to press an

---

[87] Fountain of Life, I:109.
[88] Fountain of Life, I:109.
[89] Fountain of Life, I:152-3.
[90] Fountain of Life, I:143.

argument home with God; but Christ hath the art of it.[91]

Jesus Christ taught the people the mind of God in a sweet, affectionate, and taking manner: his words made their hearts burn within them. How sweetly did his words slide to the melting hearts about him! He drew with cords of love, with the bands of a man; he discouraged none, upbraided none that were willing to come to him. His familiarity and free condescension to the most vile and despicable sinners, were often made the matter of his reproach.[92]

Others may know more in other things than you, but you are not incapable of knowing so much as shall save your souls, if Christ will be your teacher.

91 Fountain of Life, I:170.
92 Fountain of Life, I:125.

In other knowledge they excel you, but if ye know Jesus Christ, and the truth as it is in him, one drop of your knowledge is worth a whole sea of their gifts. One truth sucked by faith and prayer from the breast of Christ is better than ten thousand dry notions beaten out by racking the understanding. It is better in kind, the one being but natural, the other supernatural, from the saving illuminations and inward teachings of the Spirit. It is better in respect of effects. Other knowledge leaves the heart as dry, barren, and unaffected, as if it had its seat in another man's head: but that little you have been taught of Christ sheds down its gracious influences upon your affections, and slides sweetly to your melting hearts.[93]

[93] Fountain of Life, I:127.

No tract of time can wear out the virtue of this eternal sacrifice.[94]

Reader, let me beg thee, if thou be one of this pardoned number, to look over the cancelled bonds, and see what vast sums are remitted to thee. What canst thou do less than fall down at the feet of free grace, and kiss those feet that moved so freely towards so vile a sinner? O let these things slide sweetly to thy melting heart.[95]

Hath Christ offered up himself a sacrifice to God for us? Then let us labour to get hearts duly affected with such a sight as faith can give us of it. Do you complain of the hardness of your hearts, and want of love to Christ? Behold him as offered up to God for you; and such a sight (if

[94] Fountain of Life, I:158.
[95] Fountain of Life, I:161-2.

any in the world will do it) will melt your hard hearts. Are you at any time staggering through unbelief? Filled with unbelieving suspicions of the promises? Look hither and you shall see them all ratified and established in the blood of the cross, so that hills and mountains shall sooner start from their own bases and centres, than one tittle of the promise fail.[96]

Sinner, doth not Christ smile upon thee in the gospel? And wilt thou, as it were, stab him to the heart by thine infidelity?[97]

Remember Christ's blood speaks when thou canst not. It can plead for thee, and that powerfully, when thou art not able to speak a word for thyself.[98]

[96] Fountain of Life, I:164.
[97] Fountain of Life, I:172-3.
[98] Fountain of Life, I:173-4.

If God should damn thee to all eternity, thy eternal sufferings could not satisfy for the evil that is in one vain thought. O the depth of the evil of sin![99]

Reader, be convinced, that one act of faith in the Lord Jesus pleases God more than all the obedience, repentance and strivings to obey the law through thy whole life can do.[100]

The objective happiness [in heaven] is God himself (*Psa.* 73:25). It is no heaven to us, except thou be there. In this our glory in heaven consists, to be ever with the Lord (*1 Thess.* 4:17).[101]

[99] Fountain of Life, I:184-5.
[100] Fountain of Life, I:187.
[101] Fountain of Life, I:193.

[In heaven] the soul also is discharged and freed from all darkness and ignorance of mind, being now able to discern all truths in God, that crystal ocean of truth. The leaks of the memory stopped for ever; the roving of the fancy perfectly cured; the stubbornness and reluctancy of the will forever subdued, and retained in due and full subjection to God. So that the saints in glory shall be free from all that now troubles them; they shall never sin more, nor be once tempted so to do; for no serpent hisses in that paradise; they shall never grieve or groan more, for God shall wipe away all tears from their eyes.[102]

What a ravishing vision will this be! And how much will it exceed all reports

[102] Fountain of Life, I:194.

and apprehensions we had here of it! Surely one half was not told us.[103]

[The vision of God in heaven] will be a fully satisfying vision: God will then be all in all. The blessed soul will feel itself blessed, filled, satisfied, in every part. Ah what a happiness is here! to look and love; to drink and sing, and drink again at the fountain head of the highest glory! And if at any time its eye be turned from a direct to a reflex sight upon what it once was: how it was wrought on, how fitted for this glory, how wonderfully distinguished by special grace, from them that are howling in flames, whilst himself is shouting aloud upon his bed of everlasting rest; all this will enhance glory.[104]

[103] Fountain of Life, I:194.
[104] Fountain of Life, I:195.

Scripture knows no other way to glory, but Christ put on and applied by faith. Scripture asserts the impossibility of being or doing anything that is truly evangelically good out of Christ (*John* 15:5).[105]

Everlasting salvation is the privilege of all over whom Christ reigns. Prince and Saviour are joined together. He that can say, 'Thou shalt guide me with thy counsels', may add what follows, 'and afterwards bring me to glory' (*Psa.* 73:24). Indeed, the kingdom of grace doth but breed up children for the kingdom of glory. And to speak as the thing is, it is the kingdom of heaven here begun.[106]

Do you see your condition how sad, miserable, wretched it is by nature? Do you see

---

[105] Fountain of Life, I:197.
[106] Fountain of Life, I:207.

your remedy, as it lies only in Christ and his precious blood? Do you see the true way of obtaining interest in that blood by faith? Doth this knowledge run into practice, and put you upon lamenting heartily your misery by sin, thirsting vehemently after Christ and his righteousness, striving continually for a heart to believe, and close with Christ? This will evidence you indeed to be translated out of the kingdom of darkness, into the kingdom of Christ.[107]

The best men cannot escape sin in their most holy actions.[108]

None doth, or can love like Christ: his love to man is matchless.[109]

[107] Fountain of Life, I:209-10
[108] Fountain of Life, I:217.
[109] Fountain of Life, I:232.

He that hath a precious treasure will be loth to adventure it in a leaky vessel: woe to the holiest man on earth, if the safety of his precious soul were to be adventured on the bottom of the best duty that ever he performed. But Christ's obedience and righteousness is firm and sound; a bottom that we may safely adventure all in.[110]

From the whole of Christ's humiliation in his life, learn you to pass through all the troubles of your life with a contented, composed spirit, as Christ your forerunner did. When ye therefore pass through any of these trials, look to Jesus, and consider him.[111]

And when that surpassing love breaks out in its glory upon the soul, how is the

[110] Fountain of Life, I:241-2.
[111] Fountain of Life, I:246.

soul transported, and ravished with it! crying out, what manner of love is this! here is a love large enough to go round the heavens, and the heaven of heavens! Who ever loved after this rate, to lay down his life for enemies! O love unutterable and inconceivable! How glorious is my love in his red garments! All these ways it remembers us of Christ, and helps powerfully to raise, warm, and affect our hearts with that remembrance of him. Take thine own Christ into the arms of thy faith this day.[112]

[In Gethsemane] Christ left us an excellent pattern, what we ought to do, when imminent dangers are near us even at the door. It becomes a soldier to die fighting, a minister to die preaching, and a Christian to die praying.[113]

[112] Fountain of Life, I:264-6.
[113] Fountain of Life, I:273.

I know not what I should have done, nor how in all the world I should have waded through the troubles I have passed, if it had not been for the help of prayer.[114]

In heaven we shall meet many that we never thought to meet there, and miss many we were confident we should see there.[115]

Fear what others may do, but fear thyself more.[116]

Certain is it that out of Christ's condemnation flows our justification; and had not sentence been given against him, it must have been given against us. O what a melting consideration is this! That out of his agony comes our victory; out of his

[114] Fountain of Life, I:280.
[115] Fountain of Life, I:295.
[116] Fountain of Life, I:295.

condemnation, our justification; out of his pain, our ease; out of his stripes, our healing; out of his gall and vinegar, our honey; out of his curse, our blessing; out of his crown of thorns, our crown of glory; out of his death our life: if he could not be released, it was that you might. If Pilate gave sentence against him, it was that the great God might never give sentence against you.[117]

[Could Pilate be] free from his blood, because he washed his hands in water? No, no, he could never be free, except his soul had been washed in that blood he shed.[118]

Of all the false signs of grace, none more dangerous than those that most resemble true ones. Possibly, if thou wouldst but

[117] Fountain of Life, I:307.
[118] Fountain of Life, I:304.

search thine own heart in this matter, thou mayest find, that any other pathetical, moving story, will have the like effects upon thee.[119]

How soon would faith freeze without a cross? Bear your cross therefore with joy.[120]

As a carnal heart thinks revenge its glory, the gracious heart is content that forgiveness should be its glory.[121]

What wouldst thou have given sometimes for such a heart as thou now hast, though it be not yet as thou wouldst have it? And however you value and esteem it, God himself sets no common value on it.

[119] Fountain of Life, I:314.
[120] Fountain of Life, I:331.
[121] Fountain of Life, I:379.

God is more delighted with such a heart than all the sacrifices in the world. One groan, one tear, flowing from faith and the spirit of adoption, are more to him than the cattle upon a thousand hills. [It is as if God should say:] 'All the magnificent temples and glorious structures in the world give me no pleasure in comparison of such a broken heart as this.' Oh then, forever bless the Lord, that hath done that for you, which none else could do, and which he has done but for few besides you.[122]

It is the glory of Pagan morality, that it can *adscondere vitia*, hide and cover men's lusts and passions. The glory of Christianity lies in this, that it can *abscindere vitia*, not hide, but destroy, and really mortify the lusts of nature.[123]

[122] Fountain of Life, I:319-20
[123] Fountain of Life, I:379-80.

Is there an eternal state into which souls pass after this life? How precious then is the present time, upon the improvement whereof that state depends! O what a huge weight hath God hanged upon a small wire! God has set us here in a state of trial: according as we improve these few hours, so will it fare with us to all eternity. Every day, every hour, nay, every moment of your present time hath an influence into your eternity. Surely, our prodigality in the expense of time, argues we have but little sense of great eternity.[124]

Men do not account him a fool that will adventure a penny, upon a probability to gain ten thousand pounds. But sure the disproportion between time and eternity is much greater.[125]

[124] Fountain of Life, I:397.
[125] Fountain of Life, I:397.

If we are not fit when we die, we can never be fit.[126]

The advantages of this exchange are unspeakable: you have gold, for brass; wine, for water; substance, for shadow; solid glory for very vanity. O if the dust of this earth were but once blown out of your eyes, that you might see the divine glory, how weary would you be to live? How willing to die? But then be sure your title to heaven be sound and good.[127]

You are not certain that ever you shall attain the years of your fathers. There are graves in the church-yard just of your length.[128]

[126] Fountain of Life, I:400.
[127] Fountain of Life, I:402.
[128] Fountain of Life, I:405.

Christ's desertion is preventive of your final desertion: because he was forsaken for a time, you shall not be forsaken forever: for he was forsaken for you: and God's forsaking him, though but for a few hours, is equivalent to his forsaking you for ever.[129]

Humble your souls before the Lord for every evil you shall be convinced of: tell him, it pierces your hearts that you have so displeased him, and that it shall be a caution to you, whilst you live, never to return again to folly: invite him again to your souls, and mourn after the Lord till you have found him: if you seek him, he will be found of you (*2 Chron.* 15:2). It may be you shall have a thousand comforters come about your sad souls, in such a time to comfort them: this will be to you instead of God, and that will

[129] Fountain of Life, I:415.

repair your loss of Christ. Despise them all, and say, I am resolved to sit as a widow until Christ return; he, or none, shall have my love.[130]

If Christ complained, *I thirst,* when he had conflicted but a few hours with the wrath of God; what is their state then, that are to grapple with it forever? When millions of years are past and gone, ten thousand millions more are coming on.[131]

[The Father] heard the cries of his Son; that voice, *I thirst,* pierced heaven, and reached the Father's ear; but yet he will not refresh him in his agonies, nor abate him any thing of the debt he was now paying, and all this for the love he had to poor sinners.[132]

---

[130] Fountain of Life, I:418.
[131] Fountain of Life, I:426-7.
[132] Fountain of Life, I:430.

Whatever the law demanded, is perfectly paid. Whatever a sinner needs is perfectly obtained and purchased. Nothing can be added to what Christ hath done. He put the last hand to it, when he said, *It is finished.*[133]

Did Christ finish his work with his own hand? How dangerous and dishonourable a thing is it, to join any thing of our own to the righteousness of Christ, in point of justification before God. Jesus Christ will never endure this; it reflects upon his work dishonourably. Not 'I and my God'; 'I and my Christ did this': he will be all or none in your justification. If he has finished the work, what need of our additions? And if not, to what purpose are they? Can we finish that which Christ himself could not?

[133] Fountain of Life, I:435.

But we would fain be sharing with him in this honour, which he will never endure. Did he finish the work by himself, and will he ever divide the glory and praise of it with us? No, no, Christ is no half Saviour. O it is a hard thing to bring these proud hearts to live upon Christ for righteousness. We would fain add our penny to make up Christ's sum. But if you would have it so, or have nothing to do with Christ, you and your penny must perish together. God gives us the righteousness of Christ as he gave manna to the Israelites in the wilderness. The quality of the food was not humbling, for it was angels' food, but the manner of giving it was so: they must live by faith upon God for it, from day to day. This was not like other food, produced by their own labour. Certainly God takes the right way to humble proud nature, in calling sinners wholly from their own righteousness to Christ's for their justification.[134]

As Christ began betime, so he followed his work close. He was early up, and he wrought hard, so hard, that 'he forgot to eat bread' (*John* 4:31-2). So zealous was he in his Father's work, that his friends thought 'that he had been beside himself' (*Mark* 3:21). So zealous that 'the zeal of God's house ate him up'. He flew like a seraphim, in a flame of zeal, about the work of God. O be not ye like snails.[135]

It had been working after God by gracious desires before, it had cast many a longing look heavenward before; but when the gracious soul comes near its God (as it doth in a dying hour) then it even

[134] Fountain of Life, I:437.
[135] Fountain of Life, I:439-40.

throws itself into his arms; as a river that after many turnings and windings, at last is arrived to the ocean. It pours itself with a central force into the bosom of the ocean, and there finishes its weary course. Nothing but God can please it in this world, and nothing but God can make it content when it goes hence. It is not the amenity of the place, wither the gracious soul is going, but the bosom of the blessed God, who dwells there, that it so vehemently pants after. Not the Father's house, but the Father's arms and bosom.[136]

A husband, a wife, a child, is rent by death out of your arms: well, but consider into what arms, into what bosom they are commended.[137]

---

[136] Fountain of Life, I:445.
[137] Fountain of Life, I:453.

What shall I say of him whom they now laid in the grave? Alas! The tongues of angels must pause and stammer in such a work. He is a sun of righteousness, a fountain of life, a bundle of love. Before him was none like him, and after shall none arise comparable to him.[138]

A Godhead, a Godhead is a world's wonder! Set ten thousand thousand new-made worlds of angels and elect men, and double them in number ten thousand thousand thousand times; let their hearts and tongues be ten thousand times more agile and large than the hearts and tongues of the seraphims that stand with six wings before him. When they have said all for the glorifying and praising of the Lord Jesus, they have spoken little or nothing. O if I could

[138] Fountain of Life, I:460.

wear this tongue to the stump in extolling his highness! But it is my daily sorrow that I am confounded with his incomparable love.[139]

Who ever weighed Christ in a pair of balances? Who hath seen the foldings and plaits, the heights and depths of that glory that is in him? O for such a heaven, as but to stand afar off, and see, and love, and long for him, while time's thread be cut, and this great work of creation dissolved!—O, if I could yoke in among the throng of angels and seraphims, and now glorified saints, and could raise a new love-song of Christ, before all the world! I am pained with wondering at new opened treasures in Christ. If every finger, member, bone, and joint were a torch burning in the hottest fire in

[139] Fountain of Life, I: 460-1.

hell, I would they could all send out love-praises, high songs of praise for ever more to that plant of renown, to that royal and high Prince, Jesus my Lord. But alas! his love swelleth in me, and finds no vent.—I mar his praises, nay, I know no comparison of what Christ is, and what he is worth. All the angels, and all the glorified, praise him not so much as in halves. Who can advance him, or utter all his praise?—O if I could praise him, I would rest content to die of love for him. O would to God I could send in my praises to my incomparable Well-beloved, or cast my love-songs of that matchless Lord Jesus over the walls, that they might light in his lap, before men and angels!—But when I have spoken of him till my head rive, I have said just nothing.[140]

[140] Fountain of Life, I:460.

Whenever you come to your graves, you shall find the enmity of the grave slain by Christ: it is no enemy; nay, you will find it friendly, a privileged place to you: it will be as sweet to you that are in Christ, as a soft bed in a still quiet chamber to one that is weary and sleepy. There you shall find sweet rest in Jesus; be hurried, pained, troubled no more.[141]

If in Christ, know this for your comfort, that your own Lord Jesus Christ keeps the keys of all the chambers of death—and as he unlocks the door of death, when he lets you in, so he will open it again for you when you awake, to let you out; and from the time he opens to let you in, till the time he opens to let you out, he himself wakes and watches by you while you sleep

[141] Fountain of Life, I:466.

there. O then, as you expect peace of rest in the chambers of death, get union with Christ. A grave with Christ is a comfortable place.[142]

If [Christ] live, believers cannot die. Because I live, ye shall live also (*John* 14:19).[143]

Christ is the only lavatory, and his blood the only fountain to wash away sin: but, in the virtue and efficacy of that blood, sanctified afflictions are cleansers and purgers too.[144]

This salvation is a wonderful salvation. It would weary the arm of an angel to write down all the wonders that are in this salvation. That ever such a design should be

---

[142] Fountain of Life, I:466.
[143] Fountain of Life, I:485.
[144] Fountain of Life, I:555.

laid, such a project of grace contrived in the heart of God, who might have suffered the whole species to perish. These are such wonders as will take up eternity itself to search, admire, and adore them.[145]

If Christ died to reconcile God and man, how horrid an evil then is sin! And how terrible was that breach made betwixt God and the creature by it, which could no other way be made up but by the death of the Son of God![146]

First, examine your relations to Christ. Are you his spouse? Have you forsaken all for him? Are you ready to take your lot with him, as it falls in prosperity or adversity?[147]

[145] Fountain of Life, I:471.
[146] Fountain of Life, I:477.
[147] Fountain of Life, I:482.

Admire the love of Christ. O how intense and ardent was the love of Jesus! who designed for you such an inheritance, with such a settlement of it upon you! These are the mercies with which his love had travailed big from eternity, and now he sees the travail of his soul, and you have seen somewhat of it this day. Before this love let all the saints fall down astonished, humbly professing that they owe themselves, and all they are, or shall be worth, to eternity, to this love.[148]

So then, if God have raised in your hearts a vehement desire, and assiduous endeavour after a perfect freedom from sin, and full conformity to God in the beauties of holiness; that very love of holiness, your present pantings, and tendencies after

[148] Fountain of Life, I:483.

perfection, speak you to be the persons designed for it.[149]

[Christ's enemies] trampled his name, and his saints under their feet; and Christ will tread them under his feet. It is true, indeed, this victory is yet incomplete, and inconsummate; for now 'we see not yet all things put under him (saith the apostle) but we see Jesus crowned with glory and honour', and that is enough. Enough to show the power of his enemies is now broken; and though they make some opposition still, yet it is to no purpose at all; for he is so infinitely above them, that they must fall before him.[150]

Imagine Christ upon his glorious throne, surrounded with myriads and legions of

[149] Fountain of Life, I:500.
[150] Fountain of Life, I:518-9.

angels, his royal guard; a poor unbeliever trembling at the bar; an exact scrutiny made into his heart and life; the dreadful sentence given; and then a cry; and then his delivering them over to the executioners of the eternal vengeance, never, never, to see a glimpse of hope or mercy any more.[151]

He that judged them is their head, husband, friend, and brother: who loved them, and gave himself for them. O then, with what confidence may they go, even unto his throne? and say, with Job, 'Though he try us as fire, we know we shall come forth as gold.' We know that we shall be justified.[152]

Summon in then thy self-reflecting and considering powers. Get alone, reader, and forgetting all other things, ponder with

[151] Fountain of Life, I:529.
[152] Fountain of Life, I:532.

thyself this deep, dear, eternal concernment of thine. O let not the trifles of time wipe off the impressions of death, judgment, and eternity from thy heart. O that long word [*Eternity*], that it might be night and day with thee; that the awe of it may be still upon thy spirit.[153]

God orders your *wants* to kill your *wantonness*; and makes your *poverty* poison to your *pride*.[154]

When you are indisposed for duties, and find your hearts empty and dry, he is ready to fill them, quicken and raise them; so that oftentimes the beginnings and end of your prayers, hearing, or meditations are as vastly different, as if one man had begun and another ended the duty. O then what

[153] Fountain of Life, I:535.
[154] Fountain of Life, I:555.

assistances for a holy life have you! Others indeed are bound to resist temptations, as well as you; but alas! having no special assistance from the Spirit, what can they do? It may be, they reason with temptation a little while, and in their own strength resolve against it; but how easy a conquest doth Satan make, where no greater opposition is made to him than this? Others are bound to hear, meditate, and pray as well as you; else the neglect of those duties would not be their sin: but alas, what pitiful work do they make of it! Being left to the hardness and vanity of their own hearts; when you spread your sails, you have a gale; but they lie wind-bound, heart-bound, and can do nothing spiritually in a way of duty.[155]

[155] Fountain of Life, I:554.

Do you, therefore, ye brave youths, the hope and desire of the reviving church, with eagerness lay hold on this favourable opportunity of enriching your minds with all necessary gifts and endowments. Keep yourselves close night and day at your studies and most fervent prayers. He will make the best divine, that studies on his knees.[156]

For gifts, let them increase; but grace, let it outshine them all.[157]

The gospel requires nothing of you but repentance and faith. Can you think it hard when a prince pardons a rebel, to require him to fall upon his knees, and stretch forth a willing and thankful hand to receive his pardon?[158]

[156] England's Duty, IV:15.
[157] England's Duty, IV:15.
[158] England's Duty, IV:28.

What sadder word can the Lord speak than this, unless it be, '*Take him, Devil*'?[159]

Ah sinners, did you but know what a Christ he is that is offered to your souls in the gospel; did you see his beauty, fulness, suitableness, and feel your own necessities of him, all the world could not keep you from him: you would break through all reproaches, all sufferings, all self-denials, to come into the enjoyment of him.[160]

It is natural to men rather to eat a brown crust, or wear a coarse ragged garment which they can call their own, than to feed upon the richest dainties, or wear the costliest garments which they must receive as an alms or gift from another.[161]

159 England's Duty, IV:43.
160 England's Duty, IV:44.
161 England's Duty, IV:46.

Many presume upon that time for repentance and faith hereafter, which their eyes shall never see. And thus presumption doth lock up the heart against Christ, and leaves sinners perishing even in the presence of a Saviour. They make a bridge of their own shadow, and so perish in the waters.[162]

[The mercies of God] take you in a friendly way by the hand, and thus walk with you: Ah, sinner! How canst thou grieve and dishonour that God that thus feedeth, clotheth, and comforteth thee on every side?[163]

Why cannot those feet carry thee to the assemblies of the saints, as well as to an ale-house?[164]

[162] England's Duty, IV:47.
[163] England's Duty, IV:49.
[164] England's Duty, IV:53.

Every sermon and prayer you have sat under with a dead heart; every motion of his Spirit which you have quenched, what is this but the making light of Christ, and the great salvation![165]

Thus the goodness and forbearance of God doth, as it were, take a sinner by the hand, leads him into a corner, and says, Come, let thee and me talk together; thus and thus vile hast thou been, and thus and thus long-suffering and merciful have I been to thee; thy heart hath been full of sin, the heart of thy God hath been full of pity and mercy. This puts the sinner into tears, breaks his heart in pieces; if any thing in the world will melt a hard heart, this will do it. O, how good hath God been to me![166]

[165] England's Duty, IV:66.
[166] England's Duty, IV:69-70.

The soul of the poorest child or meanest servant that hears me this day, is of greater value in Christ's eyes than the whole world.[167]

He hath borne thousands of repulses and unreasonable denials from you: sinner, Christ hath knocked at thy door in many a sermon, in many a prayer, in many a sickness, in all which thou hast put him off, denied him, or delayed him; yet still he continues knocking and waiting. Thou couldst not have made the poorest beggar in the world wait at thy door, so long as thy Redeemer hath been made to wait, and yet he is not gone; at this day his voice sounds in thine ears, 'Behold, I stand at the door, and knock.'[168]

[167] England's Duty, IV:75.
[168] England's Duty, IV:75.

There is a knock of Christ at the heart, which will be the last knock that ever he will give; and after that no more knocks.[169]

For all the saving mercy of God is dispensed to men through Christ.[170]

In a word, the opening of the heart to Christ is that work which answers the great design of the gospel.[171]

Blessed Jesus! nothing but the strength of thine own desire and love could ever have drawn thee out of that bosom of delights to suffer so many things for the sake of poor sinners.[172]

[169] England's Duty, IV:79.
[170] England's Duty, IV:111.
[171] England's Duty, IV:113.
[172] England's Duty, IV:114.

There is nothing like love to draw love. When Christ was lifted up upon the cross he gave such a glorious demonstration of the strength of his love to sinners, as one would think should draw love from the hardest heart that ever lodged in a sinner's breast. Here is the triumph, the riches and glory of divine love; never was such love manifested in the world. Before it was none like it, and after it shall none appear like unto it.[173]

Herein the admirable grace of this heavenly suitor appears, that Jesus Christ passeth by millions of creatures of more excellent gifts and temperaments, and never makes them one offer of himself; never turneth aside to give one knock at their door; but comes to thee, the vilest and basest of creatures, and will not be

[173] England's Duty, IV:124.

gone from thy door without his errand's end. Among the unsanctified there are to be found multitudes of men and women of more raised and excellent parts, nimble wits, strong memories, solid judgments; yea, men and women of cleaner conversations, strict morality, adorned with excellent homiletical virtues, capable, if called, to do him abundantly more service than thou canst; yet these are passed by, and he becomes a suitor to such a poor worthless thing as thou art; yea, and rejoices in his choice. Here is the triumph of free-grace.[174]

How great is the blindness and ignorance of sinners that need so much entreaty and importunity to be made happy? Can you be too safe too soon? Can you be happy too soon?[175]

[174] England's Duty, IV:127.
[175] England's Duty, IV:130, 136.

O my God, I am shut up under a plain necessity; I have no other way to take. In thee only my soul can find rest.[176]

Lord I am willing to renounce and abandon all other hopes, refuges and righteousness, and to stick to, and rely upon thee only. Duties cannot justify me, tears cannot wash me, reformation cannot save me; nothing but thy righteousness can answer my end: I come to thee a poor, naked creature. This therefore is my only way, *To him I go, and if I perish, I perish.*[177]

Christ bestows himself wholly upon you, and he expects the same from you; give up all, or you will get nothing from him.[178]

---

[176] England's Duty, IV:139.
[177] England's Duty, IV:140.
[178] England's Duty, IV:142.

Christ is not the sale but the gift of God; you come not to make a bargain, but to receive a free gift.[179]

If I am the Lord's, then my time, my talents, and all that I have are his.[180]

This is the grace that gives you the soul-reviving sights of the invisible world, without which this world would be a dungeon to us.[181]

All the believer's fresh springs are in Christ. If there be but one conduit in a town, and not a drop of water to be had elsewhere, then all the inhabitants of that town repair thither for water. In the whole city of God there is but one conduit, one

179 England's Duty, IV:143.
180 England's Duty, IV:147.
181 England's Duty, IV:209.

fountain, and that is Christ; there is not a drop of righteousness, holiness, strength or comfort to be had elsewhere.[182]

Come on, poor trembling soul, do not be discouraged, stretch out the small weak arms of thy faith to that great and gracious Redeemer; open thy heart wide to receive him, he will not refuse to come in. He hath sealed thousands of pardons to as vile wretches as thyself; he never yet shut the door of mercy upon a willing, hungering soul. It is a great matter to have the way beaten, and the ice broken before thee, in thy way to Christ. If thou wert the first sinner that had cast his soul upon Christ, I confess I should want this encouragement I am now giving thee; but when so many have gone before thee, and all found

[182] England's Duty, IV:147.

a welcome beyond their expectation, what encouragement doth this breathe into thy trembling, discouraged heart, to go on and venture thyself upon Christ as they did?[183]

The grace of God is a superabounding grace. Waters do not so abound in the ocean, nor light in the sun, as grace and compassion do in the bowels of God towards broken-hearted and hungry sinners (*Isa.* 55:6-7).[184]

By standing off from faith for lack of these qualifications, you confuse the settled order of the gospel: by putting consequents in the place of antecedents, and antecedents in the place of consequents. It is as if a man should say, 'If I were cured of such and such diseases, then I would go to the

[183] England's Duty, IV: 150-1.
[184] England's Duty, IV:153.

physician'; alas, could you otherwise procure the healing of your corruptions, or the gracious qualifications you speak of, you would have no need to go to Christ at all. Nothing is required of us in our coming to Christ, but such a sense of, and sorrow for sin, as makes us heartily willing to accept Christ, and subscribe the terms on which he is offered in the gospel.[185]

O then, in consideration of the incomparable worth and absolute necessity of this precious grace, make it your great study, make it your constant cry to heaven night and day: *Lord give me a believing heart, an opening heart to Jesus Christ.* If you fail of this, you come short of the great end and design of the whole gospel, which is to bring you to faith, and by faith to heaven.[186]

[185] England's Duty, IV:160.
[186] England's Duty, IV:210.

Thy former vileness and present unwor-thiness can be no bar to Christ's entrance, because it can be no surprise to him.[187]

If opening the soul to Christ do bring it unto the suburbs of heaven, who then would not recevie Christ into his soul, and such an heaven upon earth with him?[188]

Christ delights to comfort them that are cast down.[189]

Their way to heaven lies through much tribulation; all our troubles are not over when we are got into Christ; nay, then commonly our greatest outward troubles begin (*Heb.* 10:32).[190]

[187] England's Duty, IV:213.
[188] England's Duty, IV:223.
[189] England's Duty, IV:224.
[190] England's Duty, IV:224.

Satan [says, to those whose souls are being opened], the spirit of Calvinism is the spirit of melancholy. Well, their own experiences shall now confute it, for they now taste that pleasure in Christ, in faith and obedience, which they never tasted in the ways of sin: thus that scandalous libel of the devil is experimentally confuted. They find they were never truly merry till now (*Luke* 15:24). All true mirth commences from our closing with Christ; 'and they began to be merry.'[191]

Will a king from heaven come and sup with thee? Doth he feed thy soul with pardon, peace and joy in the Holy Ghost, seal an earnest of future glory? Then thou livest at a higher and nobler rate than any of thy carnal neighbours do.[192]

[191] England's Duty, IV:225.
[192] England's Duty, IV:225.

Religion indeed denies us all sinful pleasure, but it abounds with all spiritual pleasure. Is it matter of joy to have a sufficiency of all things for the supply of every want? He that is in Christ hath so. Is it a joyful life to be a borderer upon heaven, to confine upon blessedness itself? Then it is a joyful life to be in Christ. Is it matter of all joy to have the *Comforter* himself, who is the Spirit of all consolation, taking up his residence in thy heart, cheering, comforting, and refreshing it with such cordials as are unknown things in all the unbelieving world? Christ and comforts dwell together.[193]

Whatever the comforts and joys of any believer in this world may be, yet heaven will be a surprise to him when he comes thither.[194]

[193] England's Duty, IV:226-7.
[194] England's Duty, IV:228.

What light and vain things are all those pleasures of sin, for the sake whereof you deprive your souls of the everlasting comforts of Jesus Christ? It is true, you shall have no more pleasure in sin, but instead of that, you shall have peace with God, joy in the Holy Ghost, and solid comforts forevermore.[195]

A little sin may rob you of a great deal of comfort.[196]

Communion with Christ is frequent in the lips of many men, but a hidden mystery to the souls of most men. The saints find that reality, and incomparable sweetness in it, that they would not part with it for ten thousand worlds. The thing is real, sure, and sensible; if there be truth in anything in

[195] England's Duty, IV:231.
[196] England's Duty, IV:234.

the world, there is truth in this, that there are real intercourses betwixt the visible and invisible world; betwixt Christ and the souls of believers, which we here call *communion*. It is really and truly so, we impose not upon the world, we tell you no more than we have felt. O sweet and pleasant walk! All pleasures, all joys are in that walk with God.[197]

Communion with God presupposes the habits of grace implanted in the soul by sanctification; a sound and sincere change of heart. No sanctification, no communion.[198]

Prayer [is] a duty appointed on purpose for the soul's meeting with God, and communion with him.[199]

---

[197] England's Duty, IV:236.
[198] England's Duty, IV:239.
[199] England's Duty, IV:247.

I shall show you the transcendent excellency of this life of communion with God; it is the life of our life, the joy of our hearts, a heaven upon earth.[200]

The reality of communion with God is made visible to others, in the sensible effects of it upon the saints that enjoy it. It is sweet, Christian, when the heavenly cheerfulness and spirituality of thy conversations with men, shall convince others that thou hast been with Jesus.[201]

Well then, if God hath opened to your souls such a chamber of love, where your souls may be ravished with daily delights, as well as secured from danger and ruin; O that you would enter into it by faith, and

[200] England's Duty, IV:250.
[201] England's Duty, IV:249.

dwell forever in the love of God! I mean, clear up your interest in it, and then solace your souls in the delights of it. Need I to use an argument, or spend one motive to press you to enter into such an heaven upon earth?[202]

Nothing so transforms the spirit of a man as communion with God doth. Those are most like unto God that converse most frequently with him.[203]

All union with Christ must evidence itself by a life of communion with him, or our pretensions to it are vain and groundless. There be many of you (I wish there were more) enquiring after evidences and signs of your union with Christ; why, here

[202] Righteous Man's Refuge, III:394-5.
[203] England's Duty, IV:250.

is an evidence that can never fail you; *do you live in communion with him?* Then you may be sure you have union with him. 'If we live in the Spirit, let us also walk in the Spirit' (*Gal.* 5:25); that is, let us evidence the life of grace in us by exercising that grace in a life of communion with God. When all is said, this is the surest evidence of our union with Christ; and no gifts or performances whatsoever can amount to an evidence of our union with Christ without it.[204]

The converted soul goes to prayer as a hungry man to a feast, or as a covetous man to his treasures.[205]

If there be so much delight and pleasure in our imperfect and often interrupted

[204] England's Duty, IV:253-4.
[205] England's Duty, IV:260.

communion with God here; O then, what is heaven! What are the immediate visions of his face in the perfect state? (*1 Cor.* 2:9). You have felt and tasted joys unspeakable, and full of glory, in the actings of your faith and love upon Christ; yet all that you have heard, and all that you have felt and tasted in the way to glory, falls so short of the perfection and blessedness of that state, that heaven will and must be a great surprise to them that have now the greatest acquaintance with it.[206]

And what sweeter outlet and vent to all these troubles can you find than prayer? This would sweeten all your labours and sorrows in the world.[207]

[206] England's Duty, IV:262-3.
[207] England's Duty, IV:279.

Gifts as well as grace grow by exercise. The Lord regards not oratory in prayer; your broken expressions, yea, your groans and sighs please him more than all the eloquence in the world.[208]

To sit or kneel an hour or two [in religious duties] is no great matter, but to search, humble, and break the heart for sin; to work up the dead and earthly affections into a spiritual heavenly frame, this will cost many a hard tug.[209]

The Christian shall gain that which he cannot lose, by parting with that which he cannot keep.[210]

[208] England's Duty, IV:280.
[209] England's Duty, IV:281.
[210] England's Duty, IV:287.

Eternity itself hangs upon this little moment of time.[211]

It is not the having, but the over-loving of the world that ruins us. The most zealous age of the church was the age of poverty.[212]

Your very dust is the Lord's, and the grave rots not the bond of the covenant.[213]

Creature-comforts are only accommodated comforts to this animal life we now live, but shortly there will be no need of them; for *God will be all in all*. That is, all the saints shall be abundantly satisfied in and with God alone. As there is water enough in one sea to fill all the rivers, lakes,

211 England's Duty, IV:287.
212 England's Duty, IV:304-5.
213 Soul of Man, II:601.

and springs in the world; and light enough in one sun to enlighten all the inhabitants of the world: so there is enough in one God eternally to fill and satisfy all the blessed souls in heaven, without the addition of any creature-comfort. God is complete satisfaction to all the saints in the absence (I cannot say want) of wives and children, meats and drinks, estates and sensitive pleasures: there will be no more need of these things, than of candles at noon-day.[214]

The covenant of grace is your security.[215]

For according to the measure of our delight in, and expectation from the creature, is our sorrow and disappointment when we part from it.[216]

[214] Balm of the Covenant, VI:119.
[215] Balm of the Covenant, VI:119.
[216] Balm of the Covenant, VI:84.

The special gracious presence of God is with you in the deepest plunges of distress that can befall you.[217]

The lamp of life is almost burnt down, the glass of time is almost run; yet a few, a very few days and nights more, and then time, nights and days shall be no more.[218]

One soul is of more value than all the bodies in the world.[219]

If a man has been at court, and there obtained a pardon for his life, or a grant of a thousand pounds *per annum*, and returning home should chance to lose his gloves, or his handkerchief, sure if the man be in his wits, he will not take on or mourn for

[217] Balm of the Covenant, VI:101.
[218] Soul of Man, II:586.
[219] Soul of Man, II:495.

the loss of these trifles, whilst the pardon or grant is safe. Surely these things are not worth the mentioning.[220]

There is no stopping time's swift course, or calling back a moment that is past. Death set out in its journey towards us the same hour we were born, and how near is it come this day to many of us? It hath us in chase, and will quickly fetch us up, and overtake us.[221]

What merchant will not part with an hundred pounds worth of glass beads and pendants, for a ton of gold? A few tinsel toys, for as many rich diamonds?[222]

[220] Balm of the Covenant, VI:104.
[221] Soul of Man, III:6-7.
[222] Soul of Man, III:106.

In Adam all were shipwrecked and cast away: Christ is the plank of mercy, let down from heaven to save some.[223]

Every working of corruption, every discovery made by temptation, puts some into a fright, and makes them question all that ever was wrought in them.[224]

It is with most souls as it is with the eye, which sees not itself, though it sees all other objects.[225]

[Speaking of the glory to come for the believer] Certainly my friends—that which is to be a vessel to contain such strong liquor as this, had need be strongly hooped;

[223] Soul of Man, III:221.
[224] Soul of Man, III:116.
[225] Soul of Man, II:482.

lest it fly to pieces, as old bottles do when filled with new wine. The state of this mortality cannot bear the fulness of that joy. Hold, Lord, stay thy hand, said a choice Christian once, thy creature is but a clay vessel, and can hold no more.[226]

How doth free grace make its own way through swarms of vanity! How doth it break through all the deadness, infidelity, and hardness of our hearts to do us good! Though evil be present with us, our gracious God will not be absent from us notwithstanding that.[227]

Others may have communion with duties, but not with God in them.[228]

---

[226] Sacramental Meditations, VI:391.
[227] Sacramental Meditations, VI:398.
[228] Sacramental Meditations, VI:389.

A God incarnate is the world's wonder! Here is finite and infinite joined in one; eternity matched with time; the Creator and creature making but one person! It is an argument of weakness to admire little things, and of stupidity not to admire great things. Infinite wisdom, in suiting the sinner's remedy to the cause of his disease! The disease was the pride of man; the remedy was the humiliation of the Son of God.[229]

Souls of believers never are, nor can be tired in beholding and enjoying Jesus Christ. We used to say, one thing is tiresome; and it is very true, if it be an earthly thing, it will be so, how sweet or excellent soever it seems at first; and the reason is, because the best creature-enjoyment is but a shallow thing, and a few thoughts will

[229] Sacramental Meditations, VI:412.

sound it to the bottom; and there being no supply of new matter to feed the hungry soul upon, it is quickly sated and cloyed with the repetition of the same thing over and over. But it is far otherwise in Christ; for though he be but one, yet in that one thing, all things are virtually and eminently contained, so that every day he seems a new Christ for sweetness, and yet is the same Christ still. And in heaven the redeemed shall view him with as much wonder, and love him with as much ardour after millions of years, as they did at their first sight of him. O there is no bottom in the love of Christ; it passeth knowledge.[230]

It is admirable that ever the love of Christ pitched at first upon thee; for are there not millions in the world of sweeter tempers,

[230] Sacramental Meditations, VI:459.

and better constitutions than thyself, whom it hath passed by, and yet embraced thee? 'Lord (said the disciples) how is it that thou wilt manifest thyself unto us, and not unto the world?' (*John* 14:22). Surely he did not set his love upon thee, nor choose thee, because thou wast better than others, but because he loved thee.[231]

O if the records of the mercies of our lives were, or could be gathered and kept, what vast volumes would they swell to![232]

We pretend we have trusted God with our souls to all eternity, and yet cannot trust him for our daily bread. We bring the evils of tomorrow upon today; and all because we cannot believe more.[233]

---

[231] Sacramental Meditations, VI:459.
[232] Sacramental Meditations, VI:457.
[233] Sacramental Meditations, VI:432.

The mercy of God to eternal life, or his saving mercies, are only dispensed to us through Jesus Christ.[234]

How great a pleasure is it to discern how the most wise God is providentially steering all to the port of his own praise and his people's happiness.[235]

Study the Word more, and the concerns and interests of the world less. Reduce what you know into practice, and you shall know what is your duty to practise.[236]

And thus you see what sweet communion a soul may have with God in the way of his providences. O that you would

[234] Sacramental Meditations, VI:413.
[235] Mystery of Providence, IV:340.
[236] Mystery of Providence, IV:470.

thus walk with him! How much of heaven might be found on earth this way![237]

Prayer honours providence, and providence honours prayer.[238]

Reflecting on the ways of providence is the food our faith lives upon in days of distress.[239]

If no sin were punished here, no providence would be believed; and if every sin should be punished here, no judgment would be expected.[240]

[237] Mystery of Providence, IV:439.
[238] Mystery of Providence, IV:418.
[239] Mystery of Providence, IV:415.
[240] Mystery of Providence, IV:359.

The approbation of God is infinitely better than the most glorious name among men, before or after death.[241]

The Most High is not limited by means.[242]

Prayer engageth providence.[243]

The Lord expects praise, wherever you have comfort.[244]

If the traveller have spent all his money, yet it doth not much trouble him, if he know himself within a few miles of his own home. If there be no candles in the house, we do not much matter it, if we are sure it is almost break of day; for then there will be no use for them.[245]

[241] Mystery of Providence, IV:338.
[242] Mystery of Providence, IV:345.
[243] Mystery of Providence, IV:336.
[244] Mystery of Providence, IV:394.
[245] Mystery of Providence, IV:432.

If things continue at one rate with us, we think our prayers are lost, and our hopes perished from the Lord; much more when things grow worse and worse, and our darkness and trouble increase, as usually they do just before the break of day and change of our condition.[246]

Fear nothing but sin. Study nothing so much as how to please God.[247]

We cannot understand the mind and heart of God by the things he dispenses with his hand.[248]

Every man loves the mercies of God, but a saint loves the God of his mercies. The mercies of God, as they are the fuel of a wicked man's lusts, so they are fuel to

[246] Mystery of Providence, IV:433-4.
[247] Mystery of Providence, IV:467.
[248] Mystery of Providence, IV:479.

maintain a good man's love to God; not that their love to God is grounded upon these external benefits; *Not thine, but thee, O Lord,* is the motto of a gracious soul; but yet these things serve to blow up the flame of love to God in their hearts, and they find it so.[249]

If you see the husbandman lopping a tree in the proper season, it argues he aims at the fruitfulness and flourishing of it.[250]

To have lovely and well-pleased thoughts of God, even when he smites us in our nearest and dearest comforts, argues plainly that we love him for himself, and not for his gifts only.[251]

---

[249] Mystery of Providence, IV: 438.
[250] Mystery of Providence, IV: 480.
[251] A Token for Mourners, V: 620-1.

The Supreme Being must needs be an unaccountable and uncontrollable being.[252]

The saints have their secret delights in God, their hidden manna, which no man knows but he that eateth of it.[253]

Forgotten mercies bear no fruit. A bad memory makes a barren heart and life.[254]

Alas, it was not Christ's intent to purchase for you a sensual content in the enjoyment of these earthly comforts; but to redeem you from all iniquity, purge your corruptions, sanctify your natures, wean your hearts from this vain world, and so to dispose and order your present condition, that, finding no rest and content here,

[252] Token for Mourners, V:626.
[253] The Seaman's Companion, V:382.
[254] The Seaman's Companion, V:409.

you might the more ardently pant and sigh after the rest which remains for the people of God.[255]

Ah Christian! Is not one kiss of his mouth, one glimpse of his countenance, one seal of his Spirit, a more sweet and substantial comfort than the sweetest relation in this world can afford you? If the stream fail, repair to the fountain, there is enough still; God is where he was, and what he was, though the creature be not.[256]

It is better for thee to bury ten sons, than to remit one degree of love or delight in God. The end of God in smiting was to win thy heart nearer to him by removing that which estranged it; how then dost thou

---

[255] Token for Mourners, V:628.
[256] Token for Mourners, V:652.

cross the very design of God in this dispensation? Must God then lose his delight in thy fellowship, because thou hast lost thine in the creature?[257]

If providence had alike prospered every man's designs, and set them upon a level, there had been no occasion to exercise the rich man's charity, or the poor man's patience.[258]

Reader, I advise thee, under all disappointments of thy expectations, to bless God for any comfortable enjoyment thou hast. If God give thee a smaller estate, and a contented heart, it is as well, yea, better than if thou hadst enjoyed thy desire. The bee makes a sweeter meal upon two

[257] Token for Mourners, V:619.
[258] The Seaman's Companion, V:397.

or three flowers, than the ox that hath so many mountains to graze upon.[259]

It is a vile thing for any man to grudge that time that is spent in prayer, as so much time lost in his business.[260]

That man must be acknowledged rich, very rich in grace, whose grace suffers no diminution or eclipse by his riches.[261]

God beholds with delight the good done in secret.[262]

Rest yourselves upon him when new exigencies befall you.[263]

[259] The Seaman's Companion, V:403.
[260] The Seaman's Companion, V:394.
[261] Touchstone of Sincerity, V:539.
[262] The Seaman's Companion, V:381.
[263] The Seaman's Companion, V:369.

It is thy mistake to think thou shalt be bereaved of all delights and pleasures by coming under the government of Christ: for one of those things in which his kingdom consists, is joy in the Holy Ghost (*Rom.* 14:17). Indeed, it allows no sinful pleasures to the subjects of it, nor do they need it; but from the day thou closest in with Christ, all thy pure, real, and eternal pleasures and delight begin to bear date. When the prodigal was returned to his father, then, saith the text, 'They began to be merry' (*Luke* 15:24). No, soul, thou shalt want no joy, for the Scripture saith, 'They shall be abundantly satisfied with the fatness of thy house, and thou shalt make them drink of the rivers of thy pleasures; for with thee is the fountain of life' (*Psa.* 36:8-9).[264]

[264] The Seaman's Catechism, V:339.

Go alone, my friends, retire from the world; and say not you cannot spare time for prayer; better anything else were neglected than this.[265]

The most compendious way to ruin is to forget God and cast off prayer.[266]

God will have everything fetched out by prayer.[267]

Learn the vanity of the creature, the emptiness and nothingness of the best things here below.[268]

Can the seed of sin bring forth a crop of peace and comfort?[269]

[265] The Seaman's Companion, V:358.
[266] The Seaman's Companion, V:354.
[267] The Seaman's Companion, V:350.
[268] Funeral of John Upton, VI:130.
[269] Funeral of John Upton, VI:134.

Now it cannot be imagined, that God should plant the desire of immortality in those souls that are incapable of it; nor yet can we give a rational account, how these apprehensions of immortality should come into the souls of men, except they themselves be of an immortal nature.[270]

I do confess, Christless persons have a great deal of reason to be shy of death; their *dying* day is their *undoing* day: but for Christians to startle and fright at it, is strange, considering how great a friend death will be to them that are in Christ. What are you afraid of? What, to go to Christ? to be freed of sin and affliction too soon?[271]

[270] Soul of Man, II:569.
[271] Soul of Man, II:608.

Some providences, like Hebrew letters, must be read backward.[272]

It is of trembling consideration, how many thousands of families amongst us are mere nurseries for hell, parents bringing forth, and breeding up children for the devil; not one word of God (except it be in the way of blasphemy, or profaneness) to be heard among them. How naturally their ignorant and wicked education puts them in the course and tide of the world, which carries them away irresistibly to hell.[273]

Who made me to differ? or, how came I to be thus wonderfully separated? Surely, it is by thy free-grace, and nothing else, that I am what I am.[274]

---

[272] Navigation Spiritualized, V:284.
[273] Soul of Man, III:219.
[274] Navigation Spiritualized, V:226.

And let it ever be a humbling consideration to me; for who made me to differ? Is not this one principal thing God aims at, in calling such as I am; that boasting may be excluded, and himself alone exalted?[275]

But at last Christians will arrive at their desired and long-expected haven, and then heaven rings and resounds with their joyful acclamations. And how can it be otherwise, when as soon as ever they set foot upon that glorious shore, Christ himself meets and receives them with a 'Come, ye blessed of my Father' (*Matt.* 25:34)? O joyful voice! O much desired word! What tribulation would not a man undergo for this word's sake![276]

[275] Navigation Spiritualized, V:238.
[276] Navigation Spiritualized, V:290.

For at present we are tossed upon an ocean of troubles, fears, temptations; but these will make heaven the sweeter. Cheer up, then, O soul, thy salvation is now nearer than when thou first believedst (*Rom.* 13:11). Yet a few days more, and then comes that blessed day thou hast so long waited and panted for.[277]

You can never depend too much upon God, nor too little upon the creature.[278]

As the tree falls at death and judgment, so it lies forever.[279]

There can be no solid reason for one hour's delay; for thou canst not be happy too

---

[277] Navigation Spiritualized, V:291.
[278] Navigation Spiritualized, V:259.
[279] Navigation Spiritualized, V:222.

soon; and be sure of it, if ever thou come to taste the sweetness of a Christian life, nothing will more pierce and grieve thee than this, that thou enjoyedst it no sooner.[280]

Nor are we to expect freedom from those troubles, until harboured in heaven.[281]

No more desertions, troubled
   thoughts, or tears;
Christ's full enjoyment supersedes
   those fears.
Delights of princes' courts are all but
   toys
To these delights, these are transcendent joys,
The joys of Christ himself; of what
   they are,
An angel's tongue would stammer to
   declare.

[280] Navigation Spiritualized, V:338.
[281] Navigation Spiritualized, V:219.

Were our conceptions clear, did their
   tongues go
Unto their *Ela*, yet the note's too low.
What! Paint the sun too bright! it
   cannot be;
Sure heaven suffers no hyperbole.
My thoughts are swallowed up, my
   muse doth tire,
And hang her wings, conception soars
   no higher.
Give me a place among thy children
   there,
Although I lie with them in dungeon
   here.[282]

I have eyed creatures and means too
much, and God too little.[283]

Neither doth our new birth free us from
troubles, though then they be sanctified,

[282] Navigation Spiritualized, V:292.
[283] Navigation Spiritualized, V:268.

sweetened, and turned into blessings to us.[284]

Sacred truth's thy shelter, fear no harm.[285]

A new nature will produce new words and actions.[286]

The sum is great, but if a Christ thou get, fear not, a prince can pay a beggar's debt.[287]

Come now, and knock off those fetters of unbelief; Oh set my soul at liberty that it may praise thee![288]

Henceforth be thou my Lord and Master; thy service is perfect freedom.[289]

[284] Navigation Spiritualized, V:218.
[285] Navigation Spiritualized, V:217.
[286] Navigation Spiritualized, V:314.
[287] Navigation Spiritualized, V:263.
[288] Navigation Spiritualized, V:341.
[289] Navigation Spiritualized, V:341.

Desperate is that evil that scorns the remedy.[290]

Did God [give thee a body] to be but as a strainer for meats and drinks, a sponge to suck in wine and beer?[291]

God's unspotted faithfulness never failed any soul that durst trust himself in its arms.[292]

The committing act of faith implies our renouncing and disclaiming all confidence and trust in the arm of flesh, and an expectation of relief from God only. If we commit ourselves to God, we must cease from man. To trust God in part, and the creature in part, is to set one foot upon a

---

[290] Navigation Spiritualized, V:308.
[291] Navigation Spiritualized, V:300.
[292] A Practical Treatise on Fear, III:280.

rock, and the other upon quicksand. Those acts of faith that give the entire glory to God, give real relief and comfort to us.[293]

Oh! when shall we be done with our unbelieving *ifs* and *buts*, our questionings and doubtings of the power, wisdom and tender care of our God over us, and learn to trust him over all?[294]

Worldlings of the earth prefer the dirt and dung of the world before him; and few there be among them that profess Christianity, who love the Lord Jesus in sincerity.[295]

Persecution is the evil genius of the gospel, and follows it as the shadow doth the body.[296]

[293] Treatise on Fear, III:293.
[294] Treatise on Fear, III:320.
[295] Method of Grace, II:473.
[296] Method of Grace, II:278.

The law sends us to Christ to be *justified,* and Christ sends us to the law to be *regulated.*[297]

Sanctification belongs to the being of a Christian, consolation only to his well-being.[298]

It was an excellent reply that a choice Christian once made to another; when a beloved and only child lay in a dangerous sickness at the point of death; a friend asked the mother, What would you now desire of God in reference to your child? Would you beg of him its life, or death, in this extremity it is now in? The mother answered, I refer that to the will of God. But, said her friend, if God would refer it to you, what would you choose then? Why

[297] Method of Grace, II:271.
[298] Method of Grace, II:335.

truly, said she, if God would refer it to me, I would even refer it to God again.[299]

The carnal person fears man, not God; the strong Christian fears God, not man; the weak Christian fears man too much, and God too little.[300]

By calamities God will mortify and purge your corruptions; this winter weather shall be useful to destroy and rot those rank weeds, which the summer of prosperity bred.[301]

Our most pleasant enjoyments, wives, children, and estates, like the gourd in which Jonah so delighted himself, may wither in a night.[302]

[299] Soul of Man, III:293.
[300] Treatise on Fear, III:241.
[301] Righteous Man's Refuge, III:329.
[302] Righteous Man's Refuge, III:374.

Though he afflicts us, still he loves us. Nay, though we grieve him, yet still he loves us.[303]

Guilt is a fountain of fears.[304]

To take the Lord for our God most essentially includes our taking him for our supreme good.[305]

To droop, and tremble at the hazard of earthly comforts, while heavenly and eternal things are safe, is as if a man that had gotten his pardon from the king, and had it safe in his bosom, should be found weeping upon the way home, because he hath lost his staff or glove.[306]

---

[303] Righteous Man's Refuge, III:394.
[304] Righteous Man's Refuge, III:366.
[305] The Causes and Cure of Mental Errors, III:417.
[306] Righteous Man's Refuge, III:403.

Everything you lean on beside God will shift.[307]

In God's working there is no expense of his strength.[308]

Labour after an inward experimental taste of all those truths which you profess.[309]

That which is a truth today will be a truth tomorrow.[310]

We are to act *from* life, not *for* life.[311]

We are justified and saved by the very righteousness of Christ, and no other: he wrought it, though we wear it.[312]

[307] Righteous Man's Refuge, III:404.
[308] Righteous Man's Refuge, III:346.
[309] Mental Errors, III:456.
[310] Mental Errors, III:490.
[311] Mental Errors, III:417.
[312] The Rise and Growth of Antinomianism, III:582.

For my own part, I verily believe that the sweetest hours Christians enjoy in this world, are when they retire into their closets, and sit there concealed from all eyes, but him that made them; looking now into the Bible, then into their own hearts, and then up to God: closely following the grand debate about their interest in Christ, till they have brought it to the happy desired issue.[313]

Christians fall at their Father's feet as oft as they fall into sin, humbly and earnestly suing for pardon through the blood of Christ.[314]

Faith is the grace by which we receive all from God.[315]

[313] Antinomianism, III:591.
[314] Antinomianism, III:558.
[315] Gospel Unity, III:602.

They that have found mercy, pity and forgiveness should of all men in the world be most ready to show it.[316]

Let all church members see that they have union with Christ, evidencing itself in daily sweet communion with him.[317]

Trials are the high way to assurance.[318]

Prosperity is a crisis both to grace and corruption.[319]

Is it not hard to look upon other men's excellencies without envy or upon your own without pride?[320]

[316] Gospel Unity, III:607.
[317] Gospel Unity, III:608.
[318] The Touchstone of Sincerity, V:581.
[319] Touchstone of Sincerity, V:539.
[320] Touchstone of Sincerity, V:526.

The remission of the least degree of grace, is more to be lamented than the loss of the greatest sum of gold.[321]

The more grace there is, the more humility there will be.[322]

Afflictions use to melt and humble gracious hearts; there is an habitual tenderness planted in their spirits, and a just occasion quickly draws it forth.[323]

It was the saying of a holy man under a sore trial for the death of his only son; when in that dark day God had graciously manifested himself to his soul: 'Oh', saith he, 'I would be content, if it were possible, to lay an only son in the grave every day I

[321] Touchstone of Sincerity, V:533.
[322] Touchstone of Sincerity, V:541.
[323] Touchstone of Sincerity, V:549.

have to live in the world, for one such discovery of the love of God as I now enjoy.'[324]

Look, as our delight in God is the measure of our holiness, so our delight in sin is the measure of our sinfulness.[325]

On the coronation-day, kings appear in all their royal robes, glittering jewels, and all the lustre that can be put upon them; they shine in the eyes of the people more gloriously than all that are about them. 'There is none like him, in the beauty of his ornaments.' Much more doth Christ excel all others in beauty and glory, to the eyes of those that choose him for their Lord and King. Examine and mark all the creatures in both worlds, angels and men, and they

[324] Touchstone of Sincerity, V:550.
[325] Touchstone of Sincerity, V:561.

bear no more proportion to Christ in glory, than a glow-worm to the sun.[326]

Faith is a considerate act and requires much deliberation.[327]

[Christians enjoy] joy unspeakable amidst outward troubles.[328]

Christianity is no melancholy thing, but the fountain of all joy and pleasure.[329]

The good man hates not the person, but his sin. The wicked man hates both the person of the godly, and his godliness too; yea, the person for his godliness' sake.[330]

---

[326] A Coronation-Sermon, VI:550.
[327] Exposition of the Assembly's Catechism, VI:182.
[328] Assembly's Catechism, VI:201.
[329] Assembly's Catechism, VI:204.
[330] The Reasonableness of Personal Reformation, VI:522.

And for the loss of your pleasures, by conversion to God, that is the thinnest and silliest pretence of all the rest. That is the same thing as to imagine it is to a thirsty man's loss, to leave the puddle waters of a broken cistern, to enjoy the crystal streams of a flowing fountain; for the pleasures of an ale-house, play-house, or whore-house, to be sweeter than the light of God's countenance, the comforts of his pardon, or the lively hopes of glory with him in heaven (*1 Pet.* 1:8). Poor men! O that you did but once know what the life of holiness, and dedication to God is! what the seals, earnest, and first-fruits of his Spirit are! How willingly and joyfully would you trample all the sordid pleasures of sin under your feet, to enjoy them![331]

[331] Reasonableness of Personal Reformation, VI:541.

All men commend unity, and assert it to be the interest of kingdoms and churches. They wish all men were of one mind, but what mind must that be? To be sure, none but their own.[332]

A sanctified tongue is as a tree of life. Conversion, edification, and consolation, are the delicious fruits of the lips.[333]

Grace inherent in us, and grace exciting and assisting without, are not opposed, but co-ordinated.[334]

You see what pains children can take at play, how they will run and sweat, and endure knocks and falls, and take no notice of it; put them upon any manual labour, and they cannot endure half so much.

[332] Reasonableness of Personal Reformation, VI:521.
[333] Reasonableness of Personal Reformation, VI:488.
[334] Preparations for Sufferings, VI:23.

When our work is our delight, we never faint nor tire at it.[335]

God will have his name glorified.[336]

Be humble under all enlargements: say, *Not I, but grace.*[337]

All must be derived *from* him, that all the praise and glory may be ascribed *to* him.[338]

Oh when will you learn the vanity of self-dependence?[339]

It is your own unbelief and impatiency that gives you more trouble than the condition.[340]

[335] Preparations for Sufferings, VI:35.
[336] Preparations for Sufferings, VI:34.
[337] Preparations for Sufferings, VI:67.
[338] Preparations for Sufferings, VI:68.
[339] Preparations for Sufferings, VI:71.
[340] Preparations for Sufferings, VI:57.

A weak creature assisted and encouraged by the presence of a great God will be able to do and suffer great things.[341]

Faith animates prayer, and prayer increaseth faith.[342]

He that enquires what is the just value and worth of Christ, asks a question which puts all the men on earth, and angels in heaven to an everlasting non-plus. The highest attainment of our knowledge in this life is to know that *himself* and *his love* do pass knowledge (*Eph*. 3:19).[343]

How complete and perfect a cure is Christ![344]

---

[341] Preparations for Sufferings, VI:50.
[342] Preparations for Sufferings, VI:46.
[343] Method of Grace, II:15.
[344] Method of Grace, II:17.

Until a person be in Christ, the work cannot be evangelically good, and acceptable to God.[345]

How rich and great a person do the little arms of faith clasp and embrace![346]

Righteousness by works was the first liquor that ever was put in the vessel, and it still retains the tang and savour of it.[347]

Regeneration is the term from which all true pleasure commences; you never live a cheerful day, till you begin to live to God.[348]

All the delights in the sensual life, all the pleasure that ever your lusts gave you, are but as the putrid stinking waters of a

[345] Method of Grace, II:41.
[346] Method of Grace, II:42.
[347] Method of Grace, II:77.
[348] Method of Grace, II:90.

corrupt pond, where toads lie croaking and spawning, compared to the crystal streams of the most pure and pleasant fountain.[349]

There is nothing qualifies any man for Christ more than a sense of his unworthiness of him, and the want of all excellencies or ornaments, that may commend him to divine acceptance.[350]

And upon the imperfection of the new creature in every faculty, that warfare and daily conflict spoken of (*Gal.* 5.17), and experienced by every Christian, is grounded; grace rises gradually in the soul as the sun doth in the heavens, 'which shineth more and more unto a perfect day' (*Prov.* 4.18).[351]

[349] Method of Grace, II:91.
[350] Method of Grace, II:112.
[351] Method of Grace, II:91.

No man can receive Jesus Christ in the darkness of natural ignorance: we must understand and discern who and what he is, whom we receive to be *the Lord our righteousness.* If we know not his person and his offices, we do not take, but mistake Christ.[352]

The gospel offers Christ freely to sinners as the *gift*, not the *sale* of God.[353]

Renounce not only *sinful* but *religious* self.[354]

A proud self-conceited heart will never stoop to live upon the stock of another's righteousness.[355]

[352] Method of Grace, II:106.
[353] Method of Grace, II:111.
[354] Method of Grace, II:113.
[355] Method of Grace, II:122.

The truest and sweetest liberty is in our freedom from our lusts, not in our fulfilling them: yet who shall persuade the carnal heart to believe this?[356]

The death of sin is the life of your souls.[357]

Christ is not sweet till sin be made bitter to us.[358]

Hasten to Christ in the way of faith, and you shall find rest; and till then all the world cannot give you rest.[359]

Thou art under a happy necessity to go to Christ.[360]

[356] Method of Grace, II:122.
[357] Method of Grace, II:147.
[358] Method of Grace, II:165.
[359] Method of Grace, II:171.
[360] Method of Grace, II:181.

No man that is in his wits would leave the pure, cold, refreshing stream of a crystal fountain, to go to a filthy puddle, lake, or an empty cistern; as the best enjoyments of this world are in comparison with Jesus Christ.[361]

Set yourselves to study the fulness of Christ, and to clear your interest in him; believe what the Scriptures reveal of him, and live as you believe, and you will quickly find the peace of God filling your hearts and minds.[362]

Souls never tire in the study or love of Christ, because new wonders are eternally rising out of him. He is a deep which no line of any created understanding, angelical or human, can fathom.[363]

[361] Method of Grace, II:188.
[362] Method of Grace, II:189.
[363] Method of Grace, II:207.

As all the rivers be gathered into the ocean, which is the congregation or meeting-place of all the waters in the world: so Christ is that ocean in which all true delights and pleasures meet.[364]

Christ is bread to the hungry, water to the thirsty, a garment to the naked, healing to the wounded, and whatever a soul can desire is found in him.[365]

The loveliness of Christ is fresh to all eternity.[366]

He chose us not because we were, but that he might make us lovely.[367]

---

[364] Method of Grace, II:215.
[365] Method of Grace, II:216.
[366] Method of Grace, II:217.
[367] Method of Grace, II:220.

The same hour you shall be in Christ, you shall also be at the fountain head of all consolations. O come to Christ! Come to Christ! Till you come to Christ, no true comfort can come to you.[368]

We are charmed with the present pleasure and sweetness there is in sin, but how bitter will the after-fruits thereof be![369]

Follow not the holiest of men one step farther than they follow Christ.[370]

The law wounds, the gospel cures.[371]

Let all therefore whom the Lord hath thus renewed, fall down at the feet of God

[368] Method of Grace, II:251.
[369] Soul of Man, II:581.
[370] Method of Grace, II:278.
[371] Method of Grace, II:297.

in humble admiration of the unsearchable riches of free grace, and never open their mouths to complain under any adverse or bitter providences of God.[372]

In a word, there is an intimate and indissoluble connection betwixt the mortification of sin and the life of grace.[373]

What a heaven upon earth must then be found in mortification! Certainly Christians, the tranquillity and comfort of your whole life depends upon it.[374]

O remember what a mere feather thou art in the gusts of temptation.[375]

---

[372] Method of Grace, II:367.
[373] Method of Grace, II:380.
[374] Method of Grace, II:386.
[375] Method of Grace, II:390.

Diligence in the work of God is the direct way to the assurance of the love of God. This path leads you into a heaven upon earth.[376]

The object of spiritual delight is God himself, and the things which relate to him. He is the blessed ocean into which all the streams of spiritual delight do pour themselves. The reason why so many easily part with religion is, because their souls never tasted the sweetness of it; they never delighted in it.[377]

O the blessed chemistry of heaven, to extract such mercies out of such miseries![378]

Just as a man that is fast asleep in a house on fire, and while the consuming flames are

376 Method of Grace, II:408.
377 Method of Grace, II:409-10.
378 Method of Grace, II:420.

round about him, his imagination is sporting itself in some pleasant dream, this is a very lively resemblance of the unregenerate soul.[379]

How groundless and irrational is the mirth and jollity of all carnal and unregenerate men? They feast in their prison, and dance in their fetters.[380]

Great things, both in nature and grace, come from small and contemptible beginnings.[381]

O my God, it grieves me to think how many precious opportunities of serving and honouring thee I have lost, under pretence of endangering my health! I have been more solicitous to live long and healthfully,

---

[379] Method of Grace, II:423.
[380] Method of Grace, II:438.
[381] Husbandry Spiritualized, V:197.

than to live usefully and fruitfully; and, like enough, my life had been more serviceable to thee, if it had not been so fondly overvalued by me.

Foolish soul! hath God given thee a body for a living tool or instrument? And art thou afraid to use it? Wherein is the mercy of having a body, if not in spending and wearing it out in the service of God? To have an active vigorous body, and not to employ and exercise it for God, for fear of endangering its health, is, as if one should give thee a handsome and sprightly horse, upon condition thou shouldst not ride or work him. O! if some of the saints had enjoyed the blessings of such an healthy active body as mine, what excellent services would they have performed to God in it?[382]

[382] Husbandry Spiritualized, V:92.

God is the fountain of all true comfort; creatures, the very best and sweetest, are but cisterns to receive, and convey to us what comfort God is pleased to communicate to them; and if the cistern be broken, or the pipe cut off, so that no more comfort can be conveyed to us that way, he hath other ways and mediums to do it by, which we think not of; and if he please he can convey his comforts to his people without any of them. If he do it more immediately, we shall be no losers by that; for no comforts in the world are so delectable, and ravishingly sweet, as those that flow immediately from the fountain. Is the fulness of the fountain yours?[383]

[383] Token for Mourners, V:651-2.

The very last whisper of our departing souls should be this,

Blessed be God for Jesus Christ.[384]

[384] Fountain of Life, I:258.

GLOSSARY

approbation: approval or praise
betime: early, in good time
elah: the highest note in old church music
cloy: disgust or sicken someone with excess of
    sentiment or sweetness
concentre: bring into focus or alignment
diminution: a reduction in the size, import-
    ance, or extent of something
exigencies: urgent demands
fain: be disposed to, willingly, eagerly
fancy: imagination
lavatory: washroom

loth: reluctant, unwilling

mattocks: tools used for digging

mortify: to subdue by self-denial or discipline

orient: possessing exceptional lustre, lovely, fresh, beautiful

parts: abilities, talents

plaits: a braid

quietude: a state of calmness or stillness

radicated: rooted, firmly established

remit: cancel or refrain from exacting or inflicting a debt or punishment

rive: split or tear apart violently

seat: a place or centre in which something is located

start: to cause to become displaced or dislodged

stay: to cease from a specified activity

suffer: allow

upbraided: scolded, rebuked, reproached

waft: a gentle movement of air

OTHER
POCKET PURITANS

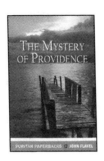

The Mystery of Providence
by John Flavel

Based on the words 'God that performeth all things for me' (*Psa.* 57:2), this book shows us how providence works for us in every stage and experience of our lives. There are avenues of spiritual knowledge and experience opened to the Christian in this work which he probably never knew existed.

'It is a wonderful book, the Banner serves us all by keeping it in print.' — Mark Dever

ISBN 978 0 85151 104 7 | paperback | 224 pp.